AF544174

# *Antje Arbor*
# *Late Vintage*

*For my 80$^{th}$ birthday party guests*

*I am much obliged to the Ross U3A creative writing group for having suggested numerous themes and topics.*

**Content**

# 1. FIVE AND TEN MINUTE SCRIBBLES

## ***Mirror on the Wall***

*"Mirror, mirror on the wall,*
*who is the wrinkliest of them all?"*

*"It isn't you, my pet -*
*as yet."*

## *A Lump of Sugar*

*A lump*
*to dump*
*into your cup*
*before you give it up?*

*Deprive yourself of sweets,*
*deprive yourself of eats,*
*deprive yourself of joy -*
*oh boy!*

*If that be all in life,*
*depriving, toil and strife -*
*where is its sweetness, say?*
*Why take it all away?*

## *Point of view*

*There is no point in telling you*
*this is my very own point of view.*
*No need to tell me why the hell*
*I shouldn't think this and it wasn't done well.*
*Why should my very own point of view,*
*I ask you, matter at all to you?!*

## *"We found Your Eye on the Lounge Floor",*

the man said on the phone. I wondered what condition it would be in now. I wondered who this "we" was. A cleaning lady? Imagine a middle-aged woman picking up what she thought was an exceptional kind of marble, pocketing it quickly, taking it home for her grandchild to play with. Imagine the man who stacked the chairs stumbling over something that felt like a pebble, kicking it away impatiently. But no, somebody had picked it up, reported the find, and compared it with the lost items book. Thank you!

## White Hair / Hare

I am the odd one out here. They think I ought to be brown. That's what the books say. The people themselves have never seen one of my kind, but they think they know better than I. A white hare, of course, is a distinctive variety of the species, and it is white for a good reason. It is only since the snow has receded to the hill-tops that my hairy coat no longer serves as camouflage. So here I am, the odd one out, an easy prey. What use is it to me that I am the prettiest hare by far? Not like all those dirt brown cousins of mine. I say, what use is this beauty to me if there is no mate in sight?

## Inevitable

Inevitable - can't be avoided. Now think of the things we think are inevitable! Wars, coffee invitations, having relatives over for meals on Christmas Day or Boxing Day, cooking a meal or two a day for your husband or partner, et cetera.

But are they? Why not just say "no"? Why not just do what you want to do? Why not just be with the people you want to be with? Why not refuse to go to war and kill and risk being killed? Why not just l i v e ?

## Odd Objects (1)

It is the length and general shape of a RULER and could be used as such, as it is made of some sort of stiff material. However, when touched at one end, it will snap and roll up in an instant to form a kind of serviette ring. If you hold it to your wrist before it coils up, it will make the most beautiful golden BRACELET, with flowers and stars shimmering and glistening as you turn it. So I would call it a BRULER.

## Odd Objects (A glass penguin)

Poor penguin! No eyes, no white colour, no mate, no water anywhere near, only cups of hot tea and coffee. It seems to have swallowed the deep blue sea, and now it looks like a glass bag filled with blue, heavy blue. Deprived of flight by nature, it is now deprived of movement even of its feet by art or artifice. Trapped in its heaviness, squatness, sadness, it seems to look up to the sky for help. This isn't me, it says. Who has done this to me? The only reminder of its origin is a narrow streak of white at the bottom of its belly.

## The Rain

No, not the reign. But doesn't it reign the country! Puddles, pools, seas, torrents, drizzles, cats and dogs - "Not a nice day today", and never is it a horrible day, and it never rains but pours. But **the** rain? Which particular rain? Rain is ever present. I suggest we write about the sunshine.

# 2. PUNS AND PLAY ON WORDS

## *Spring Things*

*It springs to my mind:*
*If we didn't have spring,*
*there wouldn't be summer -*
*what a wintery thing!*

*I'd lie on my spring-bed,*
*my spring-board for thinking,*
*I'd spring the good news*
*to the world without blinking:*

*No spring-cleaning now, and*
*white snow on the mountains.*
*No spring-onions, either.*
*All gardens with fountains.*

*Oh come, all ye tourists,*
*enjoy the new land!*
*No sunburns, no heat-strokes -*
*the new springless brand!*

## Bugs

*What is a bug? You know, I bet.*
*It crawls into the internet,*
*eats up your treasured megabites,*
*then dashes off to other sites.*

*What is a bug? Of course you know.*
*It lives in dirty beds or so,*
*emerges quietly at night,*
*your warm and cosy skin to bite.*

*It may, though, says my science teacher,*
*be just a plant juice sucking creature*
*in our garden, our field,*
*clad in a splendid coloured shield.*

*But wait, I know a tiny bug,*
*a nasty thing, worse than a slug.*
*It lives in blood and body juice,*
*in toilets, debris, slime and sluice.*

*A buggy, though this sounds quite small,*
*answers to quite a different call.*
*My toddler, all content and snug,*
*loves sitting in this super-bug.*

## *Weather-cock and weather-vane*

*From the top of the spire,*
*the world at their feet,*
*the peasant and squire*
*they cheerfully greet.*

*The beautiful proud weather-cock,*
*so nicely formed and guilded over,*
*sits on his vane, as if to mock*
*us all, for he's in clover.*

*And folk look up from field and lane*
*for guidance by the weather-vane,*
*to see which way the vane is showing,*
*to learn which way the wind is blowing.*

*The weather-cock and weather-vane,*
*though seemingly they're not inane,*
*are passive things. For they are tossed*
*this way and that, quite dead and lost.*

*Truth, constancy and active brains*
*cannot be found in weather-vanes.*
*Integrity, such lovely word,*
*a weather-cock has never heard.*

## Cuts

There is often a cutting edge to what he says. He is known for his cutting remarks, but this time they cut me to the bone. He cut me short and said he needed to cut me down to size. He said I had been seen cutting my finger-nails in the office, when in fact I had been putting a plaster on a cut in my finger. What hurts me even more is that his wife has started cutting me. Whenever I see her cut a corner now, I cut across a field to take the short cut to town in order to avoid this humiliation. I have also started cutting his lectures. So this nasty behaviour cuts both ways. I ought to cut my losses; I ought to cut the knot, to cut and run, to move to another town. I would cut it fine elsewhere. I would have my work cut out for me, and nobody would tell me I was not cut out to be a clerk. The recent budget cuts imposed by the government would not affect me, either, as I don't mind spending less. I have been used to that since my parents cut me off with a shilling. I know how to deal with power cuts and the like, too. Besides, I like sitting by candle light. I would find myself a nice little house and brighten it up with my favourite coloured woodcuts. I would plant lots of flowers and cut the grass and the hedge neatly. I would find myself another set of friends in the new town. We would sit together of an evening, cutting the cards, enjoying ourselves. I would take tennis lessons and learn to cut a ball. After lessons I would walk home through the railway cutting out of the cutting wind and out of sight of the people who might think they were a cut above me because of the old-fashioned cut of my coat and my cheap hair cut. What strangers think cuts no ice with me, though, as long as I have a few friends who take me as I am.

## Hobby-Horse

One of my hobby-horses is playing with words and finding out what games some words play with us. For example, a lady-bird is neither a lady nor a bird; a cheese-cake is not made with cheese; a Scotch egg is made mainly of minced meat (or so it says in my crossword puzzle). A faggot ought to be a bundle of firewood, but at the Ross market you can buy faggots which are tasty seasoned meat loaves.

Now take the hobby-horse. In the old days, a hobby was a small horse. Then it was an early type of velocipede. When the white man took his bicycle to Africa, the natives called it an iron horse. The hobby-horse itself is either a wicker horse used in Morris dance etc.; or a child's stick with a horse's head; or a rocking-horse; or a horse on a merry-go-round; or a topic to which one constantly returns - all of which shows the importance of horses in man's life.

Horses are stronger and faster than man. The cavalry is more potent than the infantry. Horse-power is still a unit for measuring the rate of doing work, which is 550 foot-pounds per second or about 750 watts. Even our brains are sometimes compared to the horses'. Horse sense is almost as good as common sense, namely plain rough sagacity. I wish more people had it, especially our politicians. The horse's usefulness is recorded in terms such as saw-horse; or a horse being a vaulting-block in a gymnasium; or a frame on which something is supported, as in clothes-horse. As a nautical term, a horse is a rope or bar in various uses. In mining it is an obstruction in a vein - in which case it is just the general shape and not the usefulness that has coined the term. The same applies to mare's-tail, which is the name of a tall slender marsh plant (Hippuris vulgaris), as well as of long straight streaks of cirrus cloud.

Some comparisons or likenesses are not exactly flattering, for example when somebody, especially a woman, is said to have a hors(e)ly face. Quite a number of terms imply the horse's lower status. Man is its master, the horse is only second class, as in horse chestnut - which, unlike the genuine chestnut, is ot edible - or in horseraddish - which is pungent and therefore not to everybody's taste. Some unsophisticated or base human behaviour has been given horsy names, although in most cases I am sure the horse does not deserve it. The horse may be capable of horseplay - boisterous play - but horse-trading - shrewd bargaining - is certainly below his dignity, nor can his wife be made responsible for a mare's nest - an illusory discovery.

## Never too late to have a fling (including the kitchen sink)

I'm not all that old, really. I'll have a fling at singing. Though my voice be croaking, at least I'll have fun. I'll have a fling at a Highland fling. I may not know the steps. I may not be able to follow the caller's instructions. My joints may be aching. But who cares? At least I'll have fun. I'll have a fling at painting, at modelling, at writing a novel. I can do anything I want. Who's to stop me? They may not like my pictures, my little sculptures, my long stories. It may all turn out to be kitchen sink*. But who cares? At least I'll have fun. And finally, I'll have a fling - you know what I mean. I'll have a fling at last. I'll pack everything but the kitchen sink and move to the town where he lives. I'll fling myself at him. I'll fling my arms round his neck. But will he want me? There may be a kitchen sink drama even before a wedding. And if he doesn't care about me, where's the fun?

*(kitchen sink = extreme realism in painting, drama etc.)

## Matches

It is eye-catching when a good-looking woman's outfit matches: her long skirt, blouse, handbag, shoes, umbrella, all in matching colours, hues, designs. And doesn't it arouse every woman's envy! If she is lucky, it may even arouse admiration or desire in her male compatriots. Now imagine her taking her beautiful matching outfit to a tennis-match, a football-match or whichever sport takes her fancy or that of her husband or partner. Will she still attract attention? No way! All eyes will be focused on the ball as it is projected or kicked across the turf by the racket or boot. The audience will strike their matches to light one cigarette after another as excitement rises and carries them away. The matchmakers can rejoice. Not only do they produce wooden sticks of all imaginable sizes to light people's cigarettes, cigars, pipes, candles, gas-stoves, shrines, lamps, coal and wood fires, but they may also be matchmakers of a different kind. What better way of starting a romance than a tête-à-tête by candlelight? You definitely need matches for that. A cigarette lighter would nip any romantic feelings in the bud.

# 3. PROVERBS AND SAYINGS

## ***There would be no shadows if the sun were not shining,***

*there would be no loss if there had been no friend,*
*there would be no death if there had not been life.*

*Who'd live without sun for fear of the shadows?*
*Who'd be without love for fear of its loss?*
*Who'd be without children for fear of death's toll?*

## *A Bird in the Bush*

*„A bird in the hand is worth two in the bush" -*
*but we don't eat birds now, so: quiet and shush!*

*Last summer I saw a bird brood in a hedge.*
*It was a great secret, and to that I did pledge.*
*I tiptoed to see her, I climbed on a stool -*
*but the brown lady blackbird there wasn't a fool.*
*She looked at me squarely, as if to convey*
*her suspicion of humans, whatever they say.*

*"You may not eat songbirds, but I know what you eat,*
*you keep larger birds in your yards for the meat.*
*You don't like the killing, so you buy them in foil,*
*minus head, feet or innards, leaving others to toil.*
*You cherish the meat, which you fry, grill or stew,*
*but the killers were others, and it sure wasn't you.*

*So the bird in your hand was the bird in the yard,*
*and the bird in the bush is the one that you guard.*
*I hate you," she says, "for I know you love cats*
*and the squirrels who rob our eggs just like rats.*
*My husband will still sing his song from the trees,*
*but you do not deserve it, for I know what he sees."*

## *Pushing up daisies*

*Pushing up daisies -*
*that's not for the lazies.*
*You need to be alive*
*to make the flowers thrive -*
*or so you think; but woe!*
*to graveyards we all go.*

*What lovely sight in spring,*
*when all the birdies sing,*
*a graveyard white with daisies.*
*Below, each dead one raises*
*his soil hill gently up,*
*too dead to dine or sup,*
*but still providing pleasures*
*for people that he treasures.*

## *Spilling the Beans (1)*

*Spill the beans
by all means
for all to see!
Oh do feel free!*

*Stop! All would be
devoid of mystery,
of privacy bereft,
no romance left.*

## Spilling the Beans (2)

Of course we do it all the time. It is commonly called gossiping. When politicians, a newspaper and the police are involved in it together, it is called a scandal. When an individual does it publicly, it is called libel, and when he discloses politically sensitive issues, he is likely to be jailed.

Let us return to the beans themselves. They are as diverse as the plants that grow from them. I believe in Mexico there are about thirty varieties, ranging from white to brown to green to red to black, and I have seen the most beautiful murals made entirely from beans, comparable to the well-dressing with flowers in parts of Britain. I wonder if anybody has ever thought of planting all these varieties in one garden. What a wonderful display of colours their flowers would make! You could design that garden along the lines of a baroque castle garden, you could give it a cubistic appearance, you could create any pattern with those bean flowers or paint as intricate a picture as took your fancy. If you possessed all the varieties of Mexican beans and spilled them haphazardly, the result would be an abstract painting, first consisting of the bean seeds, and later of the plants that sprout from them and of their variety of flowers.

Spilling the beans can be exciting and beautiful. Taken literally, it does not even hurt anybody.

# 4. LIMERICKS

*There was a rich man with a rocket,*
*who'd love it and cuddle it and rock it.*
*So it said: "Let me stay,*
*don't send me away" -*
*and went off in his good master's pocket.*

*There was an old woman in Ross,*
*as humble as violet and moss.*
*Her husband, however,*
*perceived her as clever*
*and called her his sweet-tempered boss.*

*A family, blithe as can be,*
*was floating atop the Dead Sea.*
*When they called a halt,*
*they were caked with salt,*
*which didn't agree with their tea.*

*A baby, the happiest of the happy,*
*was born all complete with his nappy,*
*which wasn't such luck,*
*for the nappy was stuck*
*and soon became sappier than sappy.*

*There was an old fly in a snicket *,*
*quite fat and quite lazy and wicked.*
*The young flylings shocked her,*
*her grandchildren mocked her*
*for losing all matches of cricket.*

** snicket = local term for a narrow lane in town, often between back gardens and lined with shrubs and walls and fences*

# 5. FRIENDS AND GOODBYES

## *Back from Kew Gardens*

*You said you had never seen this before,*
*a hawk with its prey – and we both stood in awe.*
*You said you were honoured to be seen by the cat*
*who came in by the window as together we sat,*

*as Bach's music, Vivaldi's and Handel's were ours,*
*with that warm autumn evening glowing like ember.*
*I made you an owl then of chestnuts, remember?*
*I made you a tiny basket of flowers.*

*You will talk to that cat, caress her, let go,*
*You'll not be responsible, oh yes, I know.*
*I made chestnut toys for a grown-up manchild,*
*for a charming wee boy who loves to run wild.*

## *To my walks leader in Ireland*

*Hello Dave, here's to you,*
*not from Dunloe Hotel*
*but from a Rhineland train*
*with a gloomy view*
*of rails, mist and rain.*
*Hope you are well!*

*To think there could be a worse day*
*than on Purple Mountain last Thursday –*
*or rather last Friday! For here*
*the world seems so desolately sere.*
*There's not a patch of blue in the sky.*
*Don't you think Saint Peter could try?*

*My heart is still in the mountains.*
*Whistle a song for me when you are up there!*

## *Thankyou to English Friends*

*I wandered lonely as a cloud,*
*content, determined, sometimes proud;*
*but when I flew across the sea,*
*a host of friends were kind to me;*
*and now my heart with sorrow fills:*
*I miss the land of daffodils.*

*(With thanks and apologies to Mr Wordsworth)*

## *To a New Friend*

*I thought I might write*
*a card from Berlin*
*but don't know quite*
*yet how to begin.*

*This place is cold and tempest-smitten,*
*few specks of colour do I see.*
*I miss the daffodils of Britain*
*and friendly walkers' company.*

## ***Goodbye to Berlin***

*All those good-byes.*
*Tears in my eyes.*
*Fingers picking weeds*
*from my own soil,*
*knowing what it needs:*
*My love, my toil.*
*Violets and crocuses, good-bye.*
*My lover is waiting in Ross-on-Wye.*

# 6. THE WORLD AROUND US

## *Water*

*Water is for swimming in,*
*being carried off the ground,*
*floating, almost flying,*
*earthbound humans' ancient dream.*

*Raindrops are for beauty,*
*sparkling pearls in the sunlight,*
*rainbow colours shimmering*
*in see-through globes lined up,*
*precariously clinging to a string,*
*wavering in a warm breeze.*

*Icicles are for winter joy,*
*snow dripping off the roof,*
*drops freezing as they fall,*
*forming candles upside down,*
*growing as they are shaped*
*into cones of cold glass,*
*all too soon slimming,*
*dripping as the sun eats them.*

## *Walls*

*Walls are for shutting the enemy out,*
*keeping your own people safe.*

*Walls are for shutting your people inside,*
*making them stay in your grip.*

*Walls are divisions in countries, in cities,*
*splitting Jerusalem, killing,*
*tearing to pieces Berlin, East and West.*

*Walls are for minding your cattle,*
*keeping the wind out,*
*safeguarding crops and your soil.*

*Walls are what makes up your home,*
*keeping your family warm.*

*Walls render privacy, quiet,*
*shutting out noises,*
*keeping your music inside.*

*Walls are for loving behind,*
*joyful, oblivious, sublime.*

*Walls are for quarrelling in,*
*unseen, unheard by the neighbours.*

*Walls are for weeping behind,*
*lonely, forsaken and bruised.*

*Walls are your hold-all, your hold-in, your hold-on.*
*Woe, if they keep out your friends.*
*Woe, if they hold you imprisoned.*

## *Trees*

*Those city dwellers, mobile talkers,*
*who travel daily as commuters*
*as paper readers, platform walkers*
*and friends of personal computers -*
*they never saw old Sycamore*
*dispensing with his two-winged fruit,*
*which travelled, as in days of yore,*
*borne by the wind, bound to take root.*

*Come spring and summer, green prevailed*
*along the rails, beside the sleepers;*
*but our city folk quite failed*
*to see a tree among the creepers,*
*that tiny sapling Sycamore*
*'mongst buttercup and willowherb.*
*All looked as pleasing as before*
*beside the rails, beside the curb.*

*Then winter raced into the field.*
*All withered, looking dead and shrunk.*
*Young Sycamore, though, would not yield,*
*showed off his little slender trunk.*
*But city dwellers, mobile talkers*
*still did not notice what they saw;*
*no paper readers, platform walkers*
*did recognize young Sycamore.*

*Next spring so green the banks did rise*
*with lovely plants, yet little known.*
*By summer then - surprise, surprise! -*
*a wood of Sycamores had grown.*

*Their roots now stretched beneath the sleepers*
*and lifted up the rails a bit.*
*By fall they had outgrown the creepers.*
*The sleepers rose. No trains! Oh shit!*

*The city dwellers were quite furious*
*to be betrayed by trees, their friends.*
*Had they but been a little curious*
*and used their brains to better ends!*

## *Too much choice*

*Christmas stalls on market day,*
*pizza, coffee, take-away,*
*hustle, bustle, shove,*
*drizzle from above.*
*There's too much choice,*
*says a quiet voice.*

*Garments, games and toys,*
*all the Christmas joys.*
*Presents - what to choose?*
*No more time to lose.*
*There's too much choice,*
*says a quiet voice.*

## Colours

My favourite colours are the colours of the rainbow. It seems they are everybody else's, too, for I can't think of anybody who will not stop and admire that beautiful semi-circle far away on the horizon, hazy yet brilliant with light split up into its components: Violet, indigo, blue, green, yellow, orange and red. Once I even saw two rainbows at once, one beneath the other. I am not a physicist and cannot explain exactly how a prism works, but the little I know does not impair my appreciation of the beauty resulting from rays of light refracted by millions of rain drops - on the contrary, this knowledge enhances my joy.

If I had a garden of my own, I would fill it with flowers in all the rainbow colours, and every month of the year I would enjoy not only a reflection of the rainbow in my garden, but in addition a multitude of shapes and inbetween colours, such as different shades of green, lilac or brown, and of darker or lighter yellows, reds or blues.

When I was a child, I felt that each number had a different colour. Strangely, I was quite definite about some but uncertain about others. Eight and four were definitely blue, a bold darkish blue, whereas three was a light green, zero was a very light yellow, almost white, and two was red. I was not so sure about five, six, seven or nine. Six may have been brown, and seven a dark lilac, but that was almost optional.

If I had to make a choice and pick one favourite colour, it would be orange. Now you would think that as everybody loves rainbows, they woud love all its colours, too. Strangely enough, that is not so.

Most of my friends and relatives were shocked when they first saw my Berlin flat after I had refurbished it. The fitted carpet in the hall and living room is a light orange, with a light orange settee to match. To make matters worse, I had painted the living room wallpaper a nice mint green. The doors off the hall all boast a bright orange gloss, and a few wall carpets in the hall take up that colour in their pattern. Orange, to me, is the colour of life and joy. It is, as everybody knows, made up of red, which is the colour of love, and yellow, which is the colour of the sun. It used to make me feel happy even on a dull day in a lonely flat. When I finally found a friend and true love and a new home, I left my orange flat behind. My friend, like most people, seems to be afraid of orange. It doesn't seem decent somehow. But he accepts me as I am and says he is getting used to my orange sweaters and blouses. I feel he has become infected by the power of life radiating from the colour orange.

## A Train Journey in September

In the First Great Western train the windows are huge, comprising almost the complete upper half of each carriage. We get a great view of the white clouds as they are recovering from the last shower and preparing for the next, with the sun illuminating them sideways, giving them a beautifully mysterious shine. They are piled up in dense, fluffy, serrated balls, forming a high silky cotton wall all the way from the horizon  to the light blue sky above our heads. The houses and trees fly past us too fast to see much of them, but a little further away we get glimpses of hilly woods, lush green pastures, hedges and brown fields. The inside of the First Great Western is blue, a differnet blue from the sky, or rather many different blues. The blue carpet is tinged with reddish dots among grey and light blue ones, which gives the impression of a slightly puplish blue. The covers of the seat upholstery are a dark velvety blue made more shiny by a multitude of very short vertical light blue stripes; four horizontal rows of wavy multicoloured lines also enliven the dark blue. As I look at the row of grey plastic seat backs and arm rests, I cannot help thinking of two long rows of bunnies sitting upright one behind the other, all of them with one ear missing and the other ear upright and very pink. Those are the plastic handles or grips for passengers to hold on to, as they walk along the passage. The overhead luggage racks are made of light dove-blue hard plastic, the blue on the walls underneath becoming even lighter around the windows and turning into a darker shade further down to match that of the seat covers.Apart from the daylight entering through the windows, the long carriage is lit by two long strips of electric lighting in the ceiling. Outside, the wind has now blown the clouds into long fluffy white ranges of snowy hills.

----------

The Eurostar from Brussels has emerged from just over twenty minutes under the British Channel. The oppressing masses of ocean water have not crushed us. Now the British rain starts pelting against the windows as if to remind us of our narrow escape from the water. Inside the Eurostar carriages we are seated comfortably in plush chairs with ear rests, which, unfortunately, are also used by people to hold on to while walking along the passage. Not as practical as the pink bunny ears of the First Great Western! The overhead luggage racks in the Eurostar are made of glass, with the rows of electric lighting directly above them. A clever idea of an elegant design. But as the luggage is placed on the racks, it hides the light, and while we are in one of the many tunnels, the occupants of the window seats have to stop reading their books or papers.

But now we are out in the open, with the sun shining, the black and white cattle grazing contentedly, the rosebay willowherbs along the railway track showing off their remaining pink petals, while inside my carriage a tired child is screaming endlessly and an irritated mother is scolding it. Soon I will be on the First Great Western again, on the way home to our beautiful, charming Herefordshire countryside and to my comfortable and quiet little flat.

## "I Never Go Anywhere."

That's what my friend INGA always said. What an appropriate name she had! When you heard her say that sentence, you felt inclined to feel sorry for her. It appeared that all she did was doing her shopping at the Ross market, supervising the servants at home and watching TV in the evenings.
A couple of weeks ago, as my partner and I went to a performance at the Malvern Theatre, my attention was caught by an attractive lady who was decidedly overdressed. You know how you don't notice individuals in a crowd - but in this case I couldn't help scrutinizing this person who seemed so much out of place there. And guess what? It was my friend Inga. I felt so embarrassed for her that I pretended not to see her, and she obviously hadn't noticed us, either. At our next get-together for a chat and a cup of coffee or two, I told her about my little adventures, as usual. I had been to Hereford to do some shopping, to Barbara's for the music group meeting, and to a most delightful performance by our local lay theatre group. "You are always so busy, going to places, meeting people and having fun", she said. "I do envy you. I never go anywhere, as you know." Well, I thought, I wouldn't call Malvern Theatre "not anywhere". But I kept my comment to myself, trying to hide my smirk.

Inga used to wear a genuine fur coat in winter. Her husband boasted a real status symbol of a car. When I told her about my latest overseas package trip, she said: "Aren't you a lucky person to have seen so much of the world. You know, we couldn't afford such holidays. We never go anywhere." I remarked soberly that everybody spends their money on what is most important to them. I could tell she didn't like that. In fact, she looked quite offended.

Last week my partner and I started on our long-looked-forward-to luxury cruise. We had saved up for a long time. We had packed special clothes for special events and dinners during the cruise, and we felt this was a special treat indeed. When we had boarded and our luggage had been seen to, we looked around the spacious ship and tried to assess our companions-to-be. And it wasn't long before we spotted Inga and her husband. Inga was wearing the most stunning outfit and had donned gold earrings, gold rings and bracelets. She certainly didn't look like somebody who couldn't afford the trip or like somebody who never goes anywhere, nor did her husband. She seemed completely at ease - until she saw me. She turned deadly pale. Then she took to her high heels, dashing towards the exit. The ship was just about to depart, the gangplank had already been removed. Inga tried to jump the gap, failed, and was swallowed up by the water. With the crowd gathering quickly around us, we were unable to see whether she re-emerged. We certainly never saw her again.

I wonder whether she will tell the angels in heaven, too, that she never went anywhere while residing on this planet.

## Steam

Steam is hot air evaporating from boiling water, or, according to my Concise Oxford Dictionary, “invisible gas into which water is changed by boiling, used as motive power by virtue of its elasticity”. This is where the steam engine comes in, of course, which uses that motive power, that power for moving things. Its invention has produced such interesting and useful things as the steam accumulator locomotive and the steam battery locomotive, which move wheels along rails; also the steam cooker, the steamer or steamboat or steamship, and the steam laundry with its steam washing machine, steam-generated dryer, ironer and laundry press; not to forget the steam-operated forging press; the steam power station, which generates electricity; or the steam organ, which is a set of whistles producing musical notes; in this case, I think, pressured steam replaces a flute player’s forcibly exhaled breath.

As our forefathers’ minds became preoccupied with the power of steam, the word steam infiltrated our language and came to be used in allegories and sayings, likening human beings to engines, such as in ”get up steam”, meaning to work oneself into an energetic or angry state; “let off steam”, to relieve one’s pent-up energy of feelings; or “under one’s own steam”, without external motive power. Steam has even become a verb. “To steam up” can mean to make a person excited or angry; steam or steam up can also mean to work vigorously or to make great progress. If you take the hot air without the pressure, it may mean excited or boastful talk, during which a person blows himself up to appear larger, as if a hot air balloon is blown up. And isn't it a nice saying, "When the balloon goes up" for when action or trouble begins!

Another word for steam is, of course, water vapour, which the Concise Oxford Dictionary defines as "moisture diffused or suspended in air, e. g. mist"; or "gaseous form of a normally liquid substance, present above it and into which it is entirely converted when heated above boiling point". But vapour also means an "unsubstantial thing, vain imagination, depression, melancholy, hypochondria, hysteria, or similar nervous disorder". When you are vapourish or vapoury, you "utter idle boasts or empty talk". I can just imagine the vapour or steam cloud evaporating from a person's mouth and nose.while he is boasting. Now doesn't that remind you of mythical beasts, such as the Welsh dragon?

## Growing

That's why we love spring: Flowers are sprouting from the hard damp soil, beginning to grow, to unfold their green leaves, their colourful petals. Shrubs and trees are sprinkled with dots of light green and end up smothered in the darker shades of all varieties of green, soothing the eye, warming our hearts and offering shade to the wanderer. Most animals, birds and insects are born in spring. We love watching the new-born lambs in the fields, snow-white dots on staggering legs among the fluffy, somewhat shaggy, almost brownish balls that are their mothers, aunts and great-aunts. House martins build their nests in our archways and underneath eaves. We know their chicks have hatched when we hear them chirp as their parents fly to and fro to feed them. Spring means new life, means growth, means hope.

A woman with child is expectant, looking forward to seeing the new life that is growing within her and will continue growing once delivered from her womb. An author is like a woman with child, his new world of thoughts turning into words and sentences and stories, and when his time has come, a book will be delivered, and sometimes he is fortunate enough to see his offspring continue to grow in his readers' minds.

Strangely enough, we seem to cherish the hope of growth more than its result. We love the beginnings - the bud, the chick, the lamb, the baby. At Christmas we celebrate the birth of a child, the hope of joy, of eternal life. We do not want to know that all growth has its limits, that it is bound to stop one day. We do not like things to end. We hate to say good-bye - to the bright colours of summer, to the songs of birds, to our children as they leave the house for good. After recovering from the deprivations of the last war, we became enthralled with economic growth. It meant eating plenty of food, it meant shopping, shopping, shopping. More clothes, fashionable furniture, fast cars, travelling. More, more, more. This still goes on. We don't want to know that growth cannot continue forever. We enjoy a balloon being blown up, slowly filling with air, expanding, becoming lighter, rising, drifting away. Or we give it to a child, sharing his joy. Older children may experiment and prick it and shriek when it implodes and shrivels: The fascination of fear and of destruction - one of the incentives for war, for the obliteration of all that has grown.

Some growths are malignant from the start. Even for them there is no hope of permanence. They are moribund like the people they inhabit and will be buried with them. Like their victims, they will disintegrate eventually, providing energy for new life and new growth from the soil in spring.

# 7. FANTASY AND IMAGINATION

## *Tired*

*Tiredness stopping my steps,*
*fatigue blocking my brain,*

*vagueness evaporating - from where? -*
*creeping into crevices,*

*sending my head spinning,*
*creating distorted dreams,*

*making reason retreat,*
*losing love on the way,*
*leaving hope in a heap of tired rags.*

## *Tree Metamorphoses*

*A chestnut tree
that I can see
outside my house
looks like a grouse,
the Famous Grouse.
A thing sublime -
but within time
it will have turned,
revolved and churned,
stood on its head,
until it's dead.*

*An apple tree
that I can see
here by my house
looks like my spouse,
my Famous Spouse.
The doorbells chime -
I'd better mime.
The food is burned -
"You have not learned!"
No tears I shed.
I feel like lead.*

*I'd rather be
a woodland tree
far from the house,
far from my spouse
and Famous Grouse.
I've served my time
as paradigm.*

*I won't be spurned.*
*Soon I'll have turned*
*and will be fed*
*with dew instead.*

## *Destiny*

*What is in store for you in life?*
*A loyal husband, faithful wife?*
*A string of lovers? Toil and strife?*

*When struck with ill or blessed with bliss -*
*you think you have no say in this?*
*Watch at the crossroads! Stay alert!*
*You have a choice, though it may hurt.*

*Though you be ill, though you be old -*
*that's not your whole life's story told.*
*You've shaped it, chiselled, formed, created,*
*you have been sad, distraught, elated,*
*you have found friendship, beauty, pain,*
*you have not lived your life in vain.*

*When life draws to its close, you'll see*
*there's no such thing as destiny.*

## *Bench Story*

When I was a child, my parents kept me hidden from view - that is to say, my father did, because, for reasons the reader will eventually come to realize, I could not stay with my mother. So I lived as a recluse high up in the Welsh mountains, where I practised climbing and grew strong and confident. On my eighteenth birthday my father presented me with a pair of Wellington boots and a woolly hat. This is the outfit in which I was to be known by the people of Ross, for I soon descended from the hills to discover the world to which ran the streams originating in our mountains. I was particularly enchanted with the River Wye, and eventually settled in Ross. Every day I took a long walk along its banks, always resting on the same bench on my return. There I listened to the birds' chatter, the people's gossip and the wind in the willows, and I sent my eyes and my imagination on a journey to follow the flow of the river until its water finally reached the sea.

Everybody who passed me on a regular basis, such as the lonely men and women taking their dogs for a walk, came to know me by sight: a woman in Wellington boots and with a woolly hat covering her head. The walkers on the Wye banks may have considered my outfit suitable enough, for the winds tend to be rough here and the river tends to rise and leave the paths quite muddy. Visitors to the town, however, when seeing me in the streets, probably took me for a bag-lady. The Wye valley walkers and I were on good terms, sharing the same pastime. We would say hello at first, later on we would stop and chat and eventually we would get to know each other quite well.

As time went by, I became a respected citizen of Ross. I made friends there, too, although they thought me slightly odd for never taking off my boots. Little did they know what was hidden beneath my Wellies. But you will probably guess when I tell you that I needed to protect the boots inside with thick felt socks, which I wore at home, too, to protect the carpet. For my father was a mountain goat.

My woolly hat became quite an encumbrance in summer. So I had a nice becoming wig made to replace the hat. It did make my head appear slightly too large, but that couldn't be helped. When I went to see friends, too, the wig replaced the woolly hat, for I didn't want to embarrass the people I liked. They were quite right in finding me odd, or, as they pleased to call it, a bit excentric. But if they had seen me at night during that rainy November of 2009, they would not have believed their eyes. It had been pouring for weeks; the River Wye had left its bed and had formed numerous lakes in the meadows and fields. The seats of the benches lining the river banks in Ross were submerged in water. The water acted on me like a spell. It wasn't sea water, but still I felt it calling me as if I were to go to sea. I got up in the middle of the night ever so often and sat on my drenched bench by the river for hours, feeling as happy as I had never felt before. I knew why: It was part of my nature to want to be submerged in water. I was closer to my mother that way. For my mother was a mermaid.

## Ability

Connotations that come to mind: Unable, disabled, able-bodied, etc. I may be unable to write comprehensively about ability, but I will try - to the best of my abilities. When we were children, we were quick to say “I can’t” when we were asked to do something we didn’t feel like doing. And mother or another adult would say: “I can’t means I don’t want to”. In an emergency, however, we are able to do amazing things.

Of course most of us are disabled in one way or another. I, for instance, was poor at sports and still am. But who wants to know when you are past seventy? My inability to perform at sports in school had nothing to do with the way my body was built. I was an able-bodied, tall, strong, well-proportioned girl, able to walk or cycle long distances and enjoying it, too. But put an obstacle in my way, and I couldn’t jump over it. Give me a sandpit 4 metres in length, and I would only jump the length of, say, one metre. Give me a ball to throw, and it would never go further than 20 metres. Make the class run a 50 metre course, and I would be the last to finish. Slow and clumsy, that’s what I was. At home mother would rub it in, calling me slow and clumsy so often that it never occurred to me that I might be able to change. It also never crossed my mind that being slow might not be such a bad thing.

Being in a hurry, as mother always seemed to be, may prevent you from listening, from seeing, from communicating, from being creative - all of them abilities worth cultivating, I believe. Sometimes it takes a lifetime to discover one's abilities. If clumsiness had been my nature, I would not have been able to climb trees for pruning or for picking apples. I would not have been as sure-footed as I was when walking in the mountains, crossing crevices and glaciers as well as any other walking group member.

Parents and teachers often believe it is their function to assess a child's abilities. Once a child has been assessed, he or she is given an identitiy which may not leave room for development, for self-confidence, for the discovery of skills and outlooks never dreamed of by his or her elders. As the child and the world around him or her develops and changes, new and different abilities may be called for. So, in my opinion, a good basis for performing successfully in life is self-confidence, flexibility and the development of as many skills as appeal to you.

## Foster Child

There he was, all on his own, unaware that he was standing in the middle of a rain puddle. Tommy's face was contorted with wrath, resembling that of a snarling dog. His new bicycle was a shambles, leaning against the garden fence, useless. This meant the end of his independence. No more racing along the pavements or - against his foster mother's rules - across the street to the pavement on the other side. No more adventures away from his foster mother, away from her ever scrutinizing eyes. Why did people have to treat him so badly? He had only gone across the road to play with his new friend. They had practised riding their small bicycles, but then that boy had provoked him, so he had jumped off his bicycle, lifted it up in anger and tried to use it as a weapon of defence. But the boy's mother had watched them from the window, and the boy's big brother had come running and had wrenched the bicycle off him and smashed it to the ground. Then the mother had told him to go home and not to come back again. She was bound to ring his foster mother and tell her everything. Oh the injustice of it all!

He had better not go back to his foster mother's at all. She would tell him off severely. The punishment would be no cycling for at least a week. That is, if the bicycle could be mended. He would have to pay for that, too, of course - punishment number two - which would mean painfully reduced pocket money, possibly for several weeks. And that meant no new toy guns and no sweets. Oh, he was fed up with this treatment, with all these harsh rules, with being in that foster family, with that woman's stern face, with not being together with his own mother and brothers and sisters, with being the odd one out everywhere. No, he had better just leave. He would find himself a hiding place.

Suddenly Tommy felt hungry. His fury gave way to self-pity. And his feet were getting quite cold, too. He looked down. And there he was, still standing in the middle of a rain puddle. Which reminded him of how on a hot summer's day in his foster mother's garden he and his foster sister had filled a plastic basin with water to play in, and how they hadn't dared go in barefoot, but put on their Wellies. They had had great fun stomping in and out of the water. And then they had fetched their toy watering cans and had started pouring water into their Wellies. And their foster mother had laughed.

Tommy's stomach started grumbling again. He thought of the food they had had at the garden party that summer. He and his foster sister had been allowed to invite four friends each. Tommy's mother had come, too, and one of his older sisters. There had been games and prizes and lots of children to play with, and he had felt quite at home. In his foster mother's home he wasn't the odd one out.

He had better go back.

## I remember when I ...

I remember when I was lying curled up in my mother's womb, all by myself in the warm dark watery cave. I was pushing and kicking the flexible walls, feeling alive and wanting out. Before that, however, I was content to remain where I was. I had no will, no ambition. My memory was that of all the creatures of the world - of a single-cell amoeba, then a worm, then a fish. I developed and changed. I felt I had so many options. When I sprouted gills, I had a feeling I might end up swimming in a warm and sunny pond or lake forever, looking for a mate, producing beautiful colourful offspring. Then my gills closed. I grew lungs, while my mother's blood provided me with oxygen. I would breathe air in future. I knew I might grow wings and sail in the sky under the sun, hunting for insects to feed my young, which, like myself, would have hatched from a hard-shelled egg. I still remember my dream of flying. I still dream of flying. But it wasn't to be. I grew four limbs. This still made me a relation of a host of animals. I might have hopped or crawled or stampeded or galloped. My skin might have grown spikes or scales or hair. I remember all the choices there might have been, had I turned out to be a different four-limbed animal. Or, more along the human line, my skin might become brown or black or yellowish or pink. I remember dreaming of all the other children I would see.

Then I was born. I was pink and all alone.

## Imaginary Forces

* "I heard a voice telling me to kill that woman", the man told the jury. "It was an authoritative voice, a demanding voice, a voice that forced me to act."

* "They dared me to jump; so I did", said the youth. "I didn't tell them I couldn't swim. They would have laughed at me. I was scared stiff, but I just had to do it."

* "God wants you to free Jerusalem from the heathen", shouted the crusader. "Come and fight in Christ's name!"

* "You will go straight to paradise", the trainer tells the chosen few. "Your suicide will kill many non-believers, so you will be rewarded by Allah."

* "I looked over Jordan and what did I see? A band of angels coming after me, coming for to carry me home", it says in a spiritual sung by Christians, and they find solace in the thought of life after death.

* A host of angels was seen and heard above the inn where an illigitimate child was born and bedded in a manger. A bright star was seen stopping over the same inn. Images seen and voices heard led to the belief that a saviour was born.

* A man who had been paralized for decades was suddenly able to get up from his stretcher when Jesus told him to get up and walk.

* Imaginary weapons in Iraq made the USA and UK start a war which is now known to have been illegal.

* The emperor's imaginary new clothes were admired by everyone because of the emperor's imaginary greatness.

* A song can move you to tears or make you feel happy.

* "I love you" is magic. Love is the greatest imaginary force I can imagine.

# Antje Arbor
# Spätherbstlese

Mauer Verlag
Wilfried Kriese
72108 Rottenburg a/N
Buchgestaltung: Wilfried Kriese
Titelbild: Antje Arbor
2015
ISBN 978-3-86812-357-9

www.mauerverlag.de

*Für meine Gäste*

*bei der Feier meines 80. Geburtstags*

## Inhalt

# 1. WIR UND IHR

## *Autorenforum*

*Autorenforum, welch Vergnügen!*
*Hier darf man ungestraft wen rügen,*
*hier darf man sagen, was man will -*
*der Autor sitzt ja vorn ganz still.*

*Des Autors Grund wird nicht erfragt.*
*Er sitzt ja dort schon ganz verzagt,*
*nicht um die weisen, selbstgerechten*
*Autorenfreunde anzufechten.*

*Des Autors Wissen und Ideen*
*darf man ohn' eignes Wissen schmähen;*
*auch zäumt man gern am Schwanze auf*
*des Lesestücks geplanten Lauf:*

*Protagonist war einst der Mann -*
*der Frau steht das nun besser an.*
*Die Perspektive gar, ihr Leute,*
*welch' eine leichte Geier-Beute!*

*Und fehlt dem Hörer die Geduld,*
*der Autor ist auch daran schuld.*
*Der Hörer greift zur schwersten Keule:*
*Er spricht von seiner Langenwoile.*

*Kein Halten gibt's nun mit Ideen,*
*und bald ist's um den Text geschehen.*
*Ein völlig neues Stück entsteht -*
*zerpflückt, zerstückt, neu zugenäht.*

## *Schillers Interpreten*

*Da hocken sie, die kleinen Geister,*
*analysieren ihren Meister:*
*Wie oft er „und“, wie viel Mal „lieben“*
*in welchem Werke er geschrieben,*
*das woll’n sie eifrig seh’n und wissen,*
*Experten alle, hoch beflissen.*
*Ergebnis: Nichts als die banalen*
*und Sinn-entleerten Durchschnittszahlen,*
*dieweil der Geist, der darin lebte,*
*dem Wort zuvor behänd entschwebte.*

## ***Großstadtleute***

*Was meinst du, was heute*
*für vielkluge Leute,*
*Volk, Pöbel, Gelichter*
*und fremde Gesichter,*
*mit denen du täglich die Stadtstraßen teilst*
*und Woche um Woche zum Einkaufen eilst*
*und Monat um Monat im Fitness-Saal schwitzt*
*und öfter und öfter im Arztvorraum sitzt -*
*was meinst du, was du wohl für all jene bist?*

*Ein Niemand im Lande,*
*ein Steinchen am Strande,*
*ein Sandkörnchen nur,*
*verwehende Spur,*
*ein Windstoß, ein Atem, ein Hauch nur für sie,*
*und kämest du nimmer, sie missten dich nie,*
*die gestern gegangen mit dir auf den Straßen,*
*die hinter dir, vor dir und neben dir saßen -*
*sag' ehrlich: Hast du sie denn jemals vermisst?*

## *Wechselgesang zum 70.(80.) Geburtstag*

*A: Kann ich dir mein Unglück klagen?*
*B: Lass mich meine Freude sagen!*

*A: Siebzig Jahre, welch Gewicht!*
*(Achtzig Jahre, welch Gewicht!)*
*B: Aber mich bekümmert's nicht.*

*A: Manche Arbeit wird zur Bürde.*
*B: Ich verrichte sie mit Würde.*

*A: Müh' und Arbeit, hat das Sinn?*
*B: Siebzig Jahre, welch' Gewinn!*
*(Achtzig Jahre, welch Gewinn!)*

*A: Ach, wie schmerzt so oft mein Rücken!*
*B: Kann mich noch nach allem bücken.*

*A: Schon wird mir das Laufen schwer.*
*B: Geh' ich langsam, seh' ich mehr.*

*A: Diese vielen weißen Haare!*
*B: Ja, man kommt halt in die Jahre.*

*A: Kaum bemerkt mich noch ein Mann!*
*B: Die sind auch nicht besser dran.*

*A: (Kaum bemerkt mich noch ein Weib!)*
*B: (Es gibt andern Zeitvertreib.)*

*A: Schau, die braunen Altersflecken!*
*B: Warum sollt' ich sie verstecken?*

*A: Schusslig bin ich schon wie du.*
*B: Ach, das steht uns schon mal zu.*

*A: Diese Falten, diese Runzeln!*
*B: Meine Falten sind vom Schmunzeln.*

*A: Ach, die Feier wird mich reu'n!*
*B: Alle soll'n sich mit mir freu'n!*

## Die Hand

Sie besteigt den Bus, der mäßig besetzt ist. In der vorletzten Reihe gibt es eine freie Bank. In der letzten sitzt ein jüngerer Mann, der seine beringte Hand auf die Rückenlehne der freien Bank gelegt hat. Die Frau steuert auf den leeren Platz zu. Der Mann macht keine Anstalten, die Hand fortzunehmen.

Wünscht er sich, so überlegt sie, dass sie sich nahe genug heransetzt, um diese Hand zu berühren?

Sie setzt sich schräg vor ihn, die Hand meidend. Als sie sich nach einer Weile umdreht, liegt die Hand noch dort, die beiden Ringe zur Schau stellend, einen mit eingelegtem Stein und einen, der aus kleinen metallenen Kügelchen perlenkettenartig zusammengesetzt ist.

Was wünscht er sich, fragt sie sich wieder und dreht sich noch einmal um. Die Hand liegt immer noch dort.

Wenig später, als er aussteigt, kann sie deutlich sehen, wie sein Gesicht vor Selbstzufriedenheit strahlt. Er hat erhalten, was er sich gewünscht hat - seine Ringe haben Beachtung gefunden.

Armer Tropf.

## Das globale Netz

Ein Mann war fasziniert von der Idee der Längen- und Breitengrade. Nur dass man sie in Wirklichkeit gar nicht sehen konnte, fand er schade. Und da er viel Zeit und überschüssige Kräfte hatte, beschloss er, diese Linien sichtbar zu machen. Er schmiedete breite Eisenbänder, so lang, wie er irgend konnte. Diese legte und schweißte er nach und nach so zusammen, dass sie den Erdball in der Länge und Breite umspannten, ganz so wie die imaginären Längen- und Breitengrade. Da sie sehr gerade Wege bildeten, wurden sie bald häufig von Langstreckenläufern, Fahrradfahrern und Surfern genutzt, die allerdings wegen der hohen Herstellungskosten dieser schmalen Eisenstraßen eine Art Maut zahlen mussten.

Weil nun die neuen Eisenwege abseits der Hauptverkehrsstraßen lagen, wurden sie auch für den Geheimdienst interessant. Er nutzte dieses globale Netz für seine Zwecke. Bald wimmelte es dort von diesen Horch-und-Guck-Leuten, denen niemand entging. Allerdings übten sie ihr Gewerbe so eifrig aus, dass sie bald nicht mehr geheim blieben. Jeder wusste sie mit Namen zu nennen.

Das Ende vom Lied war, dass sich Otto Normalverbraucher nach und nach vom Surfen auf und im globalen Netz zurückzog und, wie früher, die dazwischen liegenden Weiten der Länder und Ideenwelten benutzte, wo er frei zum Denken und Träumen war.

# 2. DRAUSSEN

## *Winter*

*Der Wind bewegt die Winterzweige,*
*sie nicken leis zu seiner Geige,*
*sie necken die Vögel, die eilig im Wippen*
*in Zweigen hin und her gehüpft,*
*vom Wind getragen davongeschwebt.*

## Bäume

(Wanderung an der Havel bei Niederneuendorf)

Zwei Bäume lehnen aneinander. Wo sie sich berühren, ist dem einen eine Beule gewachsen, die sich in eine Delle im Stamm des Nachbarn hineingestülpt hat - wie eine Nase, die sich in des anderen Wange bohrt; wie ein Mund, der sich in den Mund des Geliebten versenkt. So sind sie miteinander verschmolzen.

Einen toten, knorpeligen Baum hat man stehengelassen, nachdem man ihm die Krone abgeschnitten hat. Der Torso ist einer Ausstellung im Museum für bildende Künste würdig, denn sein kräftiger Stamm ist rundherum bedeckt von einem geheimnisvollen Relief aus Rillen und Erhebungen, kunstvoll verschnörkelt und verschlungen, wie sie kein Schnitzmeister des Orients schöner gestalten könnte. Ich möchte ihn mitnehmen und als Skulptur in meinen Garten stellen.

## Blüten

Der alte Vater kommt alleine nicht mehr so gut zurecht, und so wohnt er jetzt bei Piet.
- Piet, komm doch mal.
- Ja, Papa, gleich.
- Bring das Bestimmungsbuch mit, du weißt schon, das zweite oben rechts im Regal.
- Wozu das denn?
- Mach schnell, du wirst schon sehen. - Gut, gut. Also: Pflanzen mit freien Kronblättern. Kronblätter gleich, Blüten daher strahlig. Kronblätter 6. Griffel 1. Berberitzengewächse. Nee, nee, der Griffel ist doch zweigeteilt. Das ist selten. Also lass mal sehen. Hier: Griffel zweispaltig. Aber wo ist der Hinweis auf die 6 Kronblätter? Ich brauche eine Blütenpflanze mit 6 Kronblättern und einem gespaltenen Griffel. Das Buch kannste vergessen!
Piet steht neben seinem Vater im Badezimmer und lässt seinen Tränen freien Lauf. Papa beugt sich immer noch interessiert über seine neue Entdeckung, den Abfluss des Waschbeckens, der sechs runde Löcher aufweist, wie Blütenblätter im Kreis angeordnet, in der Mitte mit einer Schraube befestigt, deren Längsspalt sie zweigeteilt erscheinen lässt. Mit abgewandtem Gesicht zwingt sich Piet, seiner Stimme einen sachlichen Ton zu geben, und zeigt nun auf den Badewannenabfluss:
- Was hältst du denn davon?
- Weißt du, sagt sein Vater, den Abfluss könntest du mal erneuern lassen.

## *Bäumchen*

*Ein Ahornbäumchen, klein und zierlich,*
*wächst wohlbehalten und manierlich*
*nebst seinen vielen Artgesellen*
*gleich neben S-Bahngleis und -schwellen.*
*Auch Beifuß, Nesseln, wilde Nelken*
*begleiten es, bis dass sie welken*
*und kahl der Ahornstängelwald*
*den Bahnhof säumt, solang es kalt.*

*Im nächsten Frühjahr grünt erneut*
*der Bahngleisrand zur Freud' der Leut'.*
*Ob Ampfer, Ahorn, Akelei,*
*ist diesen Städtern einerlei.*
*Das Ahornwäldchen jedoch wächst,*
*die Wurzeln spreizen wie verhext*
*sich grätschend in den Schotter schon,*
*den dummen Städtern recht zum Hohn.*

*Im nächsten Jahr - ich glaub', ich träume -*
*erkennt man plötzlich viele Bäume.*
*Kein Mensch hat sie zuvor gesehen -*
*wie konnte sowas nur geschehen?*
*Indes mit seiner Wurzelkraft*
*hat unser Wald es schon geschafft,*
*die Gleise, Schrauben samt den Bohlen*
*ein wenig aus dem Bett zu holen.*

*Das ärgert nun die Großstadtleut'*
*denn keine S-Bahn fährt hier heut.*
*Das schöne Grün wird angeklagt,*
*weil es den Städtern nicht behagt,*

*dass es - wie bös und unerhört! -*
*wächst, wie es will, und alle stört,*
*die hier wie angewurzelt staunen.*

*Da plötzlich klingt's wie Geisterraunen,*
*die Bohlen bersten, alle Schrauben*
*schwirr'n durch die Luft, man kann's kaum glauben,*
*man hört die Gleise drohend krachen -*
*und alle Bäume lauthals lachen.*

*Ja, lieber Städter, hätt'st du nur*
*ein wenig Kenntnis der Natur,*
*entferntest du den kleinsten Trieb,*
*wo dir ein Baum durchaus nicht lieb.*
*Natur und Dummheit, wenn auch scheinbar,*
*sind doch am Ende nicht vereinbar.*

## Die Entdeckung

Ein Trüppchen älterer Herren, die schon seit ihrer gemeinsamen Studienzeit miteinander befreundet waren, wanderte eines schönen Spätsommertages im Brandenburger Land am Rand von Berlin. Sie kamen nicht sehr schnell voran, denn die Biologen unter ihnen betrachteten im Vorübergehen jede Pflanze genau und tauschten sich über deren Familienzugehörigkeit, Verbreitung und Nützlichkeit aus, denn das waren sie ihrer Berufsehre schuldig, und nebenbei wiederholten sie alle Artnamen, komplett mit deutschen und lateinischen Bezeichnungen, um ihre alternden kleinen grauen Gehirnzellen anzuregen. Plötzlich aber blieben alle wie auf Verabredung stehen. Am Wegrand hatten sie ein größeres, länglich-rundes Gebilde entdeckt.
„Ein Bovist", sagte der Systematiker, „aber ein untypischer. Die Haut zeigt ein ungewöhnliches Graubraun. Wo sie verletzt ist, sieht man das Fleisch des Fruchtkörpers, das durch den Alterungsprozess oder auch durch Austrocknung an der Luft sehr grobporig geworden ist." Insgeheim aber hoffte er, eine unbekannte Art entdeckt zu haben. Er machte sich eine Notiz über die Fundstelle, um später alleine zurückzukehren und die Spezies genauer zu untersuchen und zu bestimmen. Und wenn seine Vermutung zuträfe, so könnte er der erstaunten Fachwelt seine Entdeckung im Fachblatt mitteilen und in seinem Alter noch zu Ruhm gelangen.
„Ja, offenbar eine Mutante", sagte der Genetiker, „ein Bovist mit verändertem Erbgut." Schnell entnahm er eine kleine Probe sowohl der Haut als auch des flei-

schigen Gewebes und verschloss sie in einem der kleinen Glasröhrchen, die er immer mitführte. Blitzschnell überlegte er: Durch seine Beziehungen zu früheren Kollegen würde er in der Lage sein, im Labor die neueste Maschine zur Gensequenzierung zu benutzen. Wenn zuträfe, was er vermutete, so hätte er nicht nur eine neue Variante oder gar Spezies entdeckt, sondern könnte zugleich auch deren genetischen Fingerabdruck präsentieren. Außerdem, so spekulierte er, ließe sich durch flächendeckende Zählung aller Boviste in der weiteren Umgebung eine begründete Hypothese zur Mutationsrate bei Bovisten aufstellen. Er und das Team, das er zusammenzustellen hoffte, würden groß herauskommen.

Der Evolutionsbiologe blieb ein wenig länger stehen und untersuchte den Fund genauer. Auch er vermutete zunächst, dass es sich hier um eine Neumutation handelte. Aber als er ihn ein wenig anhob, bemerkte er, dass dort, wo er mit dem Erdboden verwachsen war, den runden Körper fünf dunkel gefärbte Blätter umfassten, wie die Kelchblätter einer Frucht. Dies aber war typisch für Blütenpflanzen, nicht für Pilze, zu denen ja die Boviste gehörten. Ein spektakulärer Gedanke kam ihm: Sollte es ihm gelungen sein, ein Bindeglied - ein „missing link“ - zwischen der primitiven Gruppe der Pilze und der höher entwickelten Gruppe der Blütenpflanzen gefunden zu haben? Unvorstellbar, welche Sensation dies für die Fachwelt wäre!

Der Virologe hatte etwas abseits gestanden und zugesehen. Als der Evolutionsbiologe seine Untersuchung beendet hatte, trat auch er heran. Ihm kam der Verdacht, dass das poröse Material des „Frucht-

körpers“ gar nicht organischer Natur war. Seine Augen und auch sein Tastsinn sagten ihm, dass es sich hier um eine Art synthetischen Schwamms handelte. Er hatte aber auch die fünf Kelchblätter gesehen und dass das Gewächs genau dort, wo natürlicherweise der Stängel ansetzt, mit dem Erdboden verwachsen war. Eine Pflanze also, so schloss er, deren Frucht mit anorganischem Material gefüllt war! So unwahrscheinlich dies auch anmutete, undenkbar war es nicht. Schließlich stellten die Viren, für die er ja Spezialist war, eine Übergangsstufe zwischen dem anorganischen, also leblosen Zustand, und dem organischen, also lebenden dar. Warum sollte die Natur etwas Entsprechendes nicht ein zweites Mal hervorgebracht haben? Das überträfe alles, was bisher entdeckt wurde! Chemie und Wirtschaft würden revolutioniert werden, wenn sein Fund bekannt würde. Trotz seiner Erregung gelang es ihm, seine Gedanken für sich zu behalten. Er stimmte seinen Freunden zu, dass es sich wohl um eine Mutante handele, malte sich aber schleunigst ein Kreuzchen in seine Wanderkarte, um die Fundstelle so genau wie möglich festzuhalten.

Der Philosoph in dieser Altherrenrunde war der einzige, der sich nicht äußerte. „Sic transit gloria mundi“, murmelte er vor sich hin: So vergeht die Schönheit, der Glanz und der Ruhm der Welt. Denn er hatte nicht nur gesehen, dass die Sehnsucht nach spätem Ruhm seinen Freunden die Augen trübte, sondern er hatte in dem runden Gebilde auch den einst geliebten, schönen, bunten, mit Schaumstoff gefüllten Ball seines kleinen Enkels wiedererkannt, den sie vor Jahren hier im hohen Gras verloren hatten.

# 3. BEI FREUNDEN

## *Ein Tag bei alten Freunden*

*Die Wolken rasen, Wind bläst hart,*
*durchs Feld fegt rasch der schöne Regen.*
*Durch Liebe und die Zeit gepaart*
*sitzt ihr im Haus und spendet Segen.*

## *Bei Winters zu Gast*

*Ein Haus am Harz, so nah am Winter,*
*mit Winters drin und Gras dahinter,*
*mit Blumen, Obst und Büschen vielen,*
*daneben Sand, wo Kinder spielen.*
*Ein Haus, das, wenn auch nicht die Welt,*
*so doch den Clan zusammenhält.*

*Hier hörst du, wer wann wo gewesen,*
*wer krank war und auch wer genesen,*
*wer von der Erde Abschied nahm*
*und wer als neuer Bürger kam.*
*Hier findest du Bett, Brot und Wein;*
*du dankst und kehrst bald wieder ein.*

## *Zu Gast bei Grimms*

*Für Stuhl, Serviette und Benimm*
*sorgt ER mit Ironie und Grimm.*
*SIE findet das auch gar nicht schlimm.*

*Die Hausfrau sorgt für's Wohlbehagen*
*der Seele, Augen, Beine, Magen.*
*Der Gast darf kaum mal danke sagen.*

*Doch tu' ich's jetzt mit lauter Stimm'*
*und ohne viel danach zu fragen:*
*Ein Hoch dem Ehepaare Grimm,*
*die mich mit viel Geduld ertragen!*

# Vaters Wohnung

*Hier wohnt mein Kind. Doch seine Mutter*
*ist mit ihm einfach fortgegangen.*

*Im Flur ein gelber Schäfchenkopf aus Holz*
*ruft noch nach meinem Sohn, die Jacke*
*darunter wieder aufzuhängen.*
*Und an der Badezimmertür*
*da planschen lustig dicke Kinder*
*in einer Wanne aus Papier.*
*Die Enten kleben an den Kacheln,*
*alle Schwänzchen in der Höh.*
*Da liegt Kids Zahngel, Bübchen Wasch Schaum,*
*mit und ohne Erdbeerduft;*
*für Kinderzähne eine Bürste*
*mit winz'gem Kopf, am Stiel mit Sauriern,*
*mit Sonne, Mond und vielen Sternen.*
*Das Badetuch mit der Kapuze,*
*bestickt mit Tiger, Bär und Bienchen,*
*wartet auf sein nasses Haar.*

*Hier wohnt mein Sohn, doch seine Mutter*
*hat ihn aus Eigennutz entführt.*

*In meinem Arbeitszimmer stehen*
*zwei kleine Schuhe und drei Stiefel;*
*im Wohnraum noch das Babykörbchen,*
*aus Rohr geflochten, und die Trommel;*
*ein Zuckerosterhase in der Küche*
*mit abgebrochnem Kopf, und gleich daneben*
*noch der Geburtstagsring aus buntem Holz*
*mit sechs schon angebrauchten kleinen Kerzen.*

*Tagtäglich an der Kinderzimmertür*
*begrüßen mich die Sesamstraßen-Poster.*
*Der große dicke Elch ist hiergeblieben*
*und hat sich auf dem Boden breit gemacht.*
*Regale quellen noch von Spielzeug über,*
*ein Fußball wartet, Jacken, Bettbezüge.*
*Sogar ein Kinderbett ist wieder hier,*
*ein guter Freund hat mir's für dich gegeben.*
*Am Fenster kleben fröhlich deine Bilder.*

*Wenn du dann kommst auf richterlichen Spruch,*
*bist du bei mir willkommen, ganz wie früher.*

## *Wie ich zu einem Bergführerkuss kam*

*Auf eure ach so brennenden Fragen
kann ich euch heute lediglich sagen:
Der Bergführer muss etwas älter sein,
zu Hause lässt man die Kinderlein,
und wacker marschiert man mit sicherem Tritt
und hält mit den Jüngeren mutig Schritt.
Erst reicht er ein Sträusslein von Enzian,
„Weil Sie so brav gewandert san";
und gibst du dich weiter natürlich und rau,
unterlässt er allmählich auch das „Gnä' Frau".
Erst bei Überreichung der Goldmedaille –
so lange zögert die Kanaille! –
erlangst du als allerhöchsten Genuss
den stoppelbärtigen Wangenkuss.*

## *Ein Volkstanzlehrer wird 60*

*Der Gunter, ja der Gunter*
*macht müde Beine munter.*
*Heut wird er ein gesetzter Mann,*
*doch immer treibt er uns noch an:*
*Eins rechts, eins links, eins fallenlassen –*
*nein, nein, das könnte euch so passen!*
*Schere, Box und Wechselschritt –*
*kommt ihr mir auch alle mit?*
*Mit der Tanzbegeisterung*
*hält er uns ganz schön in Schwung.*
*Ach, nach einer Pause lechz' ich!*
*Kommt bald. Heute wird er sechzig.*

# 4. SEHNSUCHT

## *Heiratsannoncen*

*Tobias Knopp fand Dorothee*
*in seiner Stadt - trotz Ferneweh.*

*Studierte - unverbildet, offen -*
*wagt immer noch auf Mann zu hoffen,*
*der dies verträgt und Anfang vierzig*
*wie sie. Auch ist ihr noch gelegen*
*an - nicht zu großem - Kindersegen.*
*Wer fühlt sich nicht zu alt dazu?*
*Sie sehen fort? Grad Sie? Nanu!*

*Studierte - unverbildet, offen -*
*wagt immer noch auf Mann zu hoffen,*
*der dies verträgt und Anfang vierzig*
*wie sie. Ein alter Wein ist würzig,*
*mitunter schal; dies zu entscheiden,*
*muss man versuchen und nicht meiden.*

*Studierte - unverbildet, offen -*
*wagt immer noch auf Mann zu hoffen,*
*der dies verträgt und Anfang sechzig*
*wie sie. Denn so ein alter Wein*
*muss ja noch nicht vergoren sein.*

## *Keine Worte mehr*

*Ich habe keine Worte mehr*
*als nur noch diese: Komm doch her*
*und bleibe, um mich zu erkennen,*
*beim Namen mich vertraut zu nennen.*
*Und nenn' ich deinen, trau mir an,*
*wie ich dein Herz erwärmen kann.*
*O komm doch bald, sei mein Gesell.*
*Die Jahre eilen gar zu schnell.*

## *Dein Lachen*

*Mit deinem Lachen, deinem Scherzen*
*berührst du, bis sie leise klingen,*
*die Stimmbänder in meinem Herzen.*
*Du lässt sie weinen, lachen, singen.*

*Ich wünschte mir, dass, was da klingt,*
*bis hin zu deinem Herzen dringt.*

# *Realitätsbezogene Liebesspekulation*

*Ich denke oft, wie das wohl wäre,*
*wenn wir so beieinander säßen*
*und unsern Fraß gemeinsam äßen,*
*den ich mehr schlecht als recht gekocht,*
*den du vielleicht nicht recht gemocht.*
*Das käm' der Liebe in die Quere.*

*Auch dass ich alt bin, macht mir Sorgen.*
*Vielleicht könnt' ich dir nicht genügen*
*beim so ersehnten Sex-Vergnügen.*
*Ich denke, was du von dem alten*
*verwelkten Körper würdest halten*
*und dem Gesicht, verquoll'n am Morgen.*

*Und - schlimmstes Unglück - wenn wir beide*
*gemeinsam lebten, doch getrennt,*
*weil jeder sich in das verrennt,*
*was ihm das Leben angetan*
*und was er jetzt nicht haben kann,*
*im Lieben nicht und nicht im Leide.*

*Lass uns gemeinsam essen gehen,*
*lass uns entdecken, was es gibt,*
*was jeder auftischt, wenn er liebt.*
*Lass uns am Leben freu'n, entdecken,*
*wer wir denn sind, und nichts verstecken.*
*Und lass uns sagen: Du bist schön.*

## *Jahreswechsel*

*Ach ja, nun ist es Mitternacht,*
*und Neujahr bricht herein.*
*Ich hätt' es mir so schön gedacht,*
*mit dir dabei zu sein.*

*Ich denke mir, wo du auch bist,*
*dass du den Lärm nicht magst,*
*wie ich die Zweisamkeit vermisst*
*und das, wie ich, nicht sagst.*

*Nun wird mit Krach dem alten Jahr*
*das Böse ausgetrieben.*
*Was fröhlich und was zärtlich war,*
*ist hoffentlich geblieben.*

*Ich wünsch' mir deine Fröhlichkeit*
*und deinen lieben Blick*
*in dieser neu begonnenen Zeit*
*für immer neu zurück.*

*Ich wünsch' dir, dass der Zahn der Zeit*
*an rauer Schale nagt*
*und dass dein Herz statt Traurigkeit*
*neue Liebe wagt.*

## *Warten*

*Nun zaubere ich in dich hinein
all meine Wünsche, mein Verlangen.
Kehrtest du wirklich bei mir ein,
was wüssten wir damit anzufangen?*

*Was weiß ich von dir? Und kenne ich dich?
Wer bin ich für dich? Und wirst du mich fragen?
Was glaubst du? Was denkst du? Und kennst du mich?
Wie sollten wir diese Fremdheit ertragen?*

*Wenn du mich küsstest, so wär' ich verloren.
Ich bin es ja jetzt schon. So lange schon.
Ach hättest du mich als dein Lieb erkoren!
Dein Schweigen spricht meiner Sehnsucht Hohn.*

## ***Komm zu mir***

*Komm zu mir und liebe mich,*
*bleib für immer bei mir,*
*lieb mich ganz und lieb mich gut.*
*Ganz von Herzen lieb ich dich,*
*Trost und Freude sei mir,*
*der in meinem Herzen ruht.*

## ***Nichts als Begehren?***

*Ich weiß ja, dass du mich begehrst -*
*vielleicht als eine von sieben.*
*Möchte ich denn, dass du anders wärst?*
*Und könntest du mich dann lieben?*

*Du weißt nun, dass ich dich begehre,*
*und weißt nichts damit anzufangen.*
*Wünschst du dir, dass ich anders wäre?*
*Wärst du dann mit mir ausgegangen?*

*Du weißt ja gar nicht, wie ich bin.*
*Man sieht nur mit dem Herzen gut.*
*So sieh doch mal genauer hin,*
*mit Liebe, Freude und viel Mut!*

*Ich wünsch mir, dass zu dem Begehren*
*die Liebe sich hinzugesellt.*
*Was können mich die andern scheren!*
*Du bist es, der mir so gefällt.*